GETTING INTO

To[illegible]m

VERITE REILY COLLINS

TROTMAN

Getting into Tourism
This first edition published in 1999
by Trotman & Company Ltd
2 The Green, Richmond, Surrey TW9 1PL

British Library Cataloguing in Publication Data
A catalogue record for this book is available from the British Library.
ISBN 0 85660 459 3

Printed and bound in Great Britain
by Creative Print & Design (Wales) Ltd

CONTENTS

About the Author		iv
Introduction		1
1	Business Tourism	3
2	Hospitality	8
3	Looking After People	14
4	Museums & Attractions	20
5	Niche Tourism & Conservation	23
6	Sports Tourism	27
7	Tour Operators	31
8	Tourist Boards	37
9	Transport	43
10	Your Own Business	52
11	Invest in Yourself	59
Glossary		64
Further Information		66
Index		72

ABOUT THE AUTHOR

Verité Reily Collins worked in tourism for over 20 years, eventually setting up the largest freelance tourism booking agency in Europe. Working for over 500 companies worldwide, she devised tourism courses to train staff to look after today's demanding travellers. These courses were held in the UK, France, Netherlands, Belgium, and Bulgaria, etc. The United Nations bought her training courses, and eventually she sold her company to Sight and Sound Education Ltd.

Now working as a travel writer, she still retains an interest in tourism training, serving on the Council of ACE, involved in developing NVQs and GNVQs, and as a Director of the Tourism Training Organisation.

INTRODUCTION

Welcome to the world of tourism – one of the largest and fastest growing industries in the world. About 2.5 million people work in the tourism industry in Britain. It can provide a fascinating career, and it is possible to travel the world while being paid to work.

However, there is a downside. Most of the companies in this industry are SMEs (small and medium-sized enterprises). When applying for jobs it can mean contacting many companies. For every huge company such as Thomas Cook, Kuoni or Thomsons, there are hundreds of small companies employing two or three people at most, with no recognised way into employment. When announcements are made by government agencies about job creation in the tourism industry, these often refer to the fast-food industry with low-paid catering jobs.

In tourism you are in a service industry. Working hours are often extended if there is a crisis, a strike or delay. There are jobs working behind the scenes where hours are 9–5, but if you like meeting people you have to be prepared to work when they need you. Brussels' Working Time Regulations are not expected to have much impact; if there is a crisis and 200 delegates are arriving the next morning, you work throughout the night to sort it out. Everyone works the same hours, and probably more women head companies in this sector than any other.

Working in tourism means being prepared to go out and work at finding a job. You may have to contact over a hundred SMEs before you find one with a job vacancy. Competing for jobs with other hopefuls, it's a case of coming up with something extra. Specialist knowledge can give you the edge when applying for a job. Work experience is always helpful, and there are plenty of opportunities from stewarding at a local pop concert to helping run a charity flag day.

On the plus side, once you have your first job it is easy to move to another company as you work your way up the career ladder. Recognising it is difficult to advance in a small or family run firm, the industry regards company-hopping as acceptable career moves. Although some companies conduct very business-like interviews, you are just as likely to be offered a full-time career in a five-minute chat over a cup of coffee.

You may have to live out of a suitcase, but you don't have to do the housework or washing up in hotels; you eat in wonderful restaurants and your job could involve working at Wimbledon, seeing an eclipse or meeting MPs and film stars; all the while being paid to travel the world.

Training is never wasted, and for many specialised areas such as tour managing and guiding you have to take a recognised course. However, a recent government-funded report from the Business Tourism Forum said 'Degree courses, offered by college and universities, produce management graduates but not the range of skills and levels needed for the "nuts and bolts" of the industry'.

The report highlighted the need to focus on a 'bottom up' approach for training. In other words, get good basic training, ensure your teachers/lecturers have worked in the industry, and either take on-the-job training courses or courses in between jobs. Basic training should include first aid. Travel geography is useful. Although 80% of the world's tourism industry uses English, languages are always useful.

Often a good marketing or business management course is more acceptable than a tourism qualification. If you do take GNVQs, NVQs, HNDs or a tourism degree, the most important factor is to ask if the lecturers have worked in the industry. And if you are fobbed off, find another college.

In *Getting into Tourism* we hope to explain about the industry and how you too can be part of this hard-working, sometimes frustrating, vibrant, exciting and glamorous world. There is competition to get into the industry, so we have highlighted some of the lesser-known jobs where there are just as many opportunities but less competition. We hope this book starts you on the way to a fulfilling career.

Enjoy it!

Chapter 1
BUSINESS TOURISM

This is the top end of the tourism industry, consisting of conferences, exhibitions, incentive travel, corporate hospitality and individual business travel. Although only a small part of the industry, it accounts for some 29% of all inbound tourism expenditure, growing faster than leisure tourism.

There is work for freelance and full-time staff. Often someone will work as a freelance receptionist or interpreter at an exhibition or conference, then go on to work at different events, usually in the UK but sometimes abroad. Eventually a company may offer a full-time job in organisation or administration when a vacancy occurs.

Types of job

- Administration and organising staff
- Interpreters
- Receptionists
- 'Backroom' staff for driving, erecting stands, carpentry
- Logistics
- Stewards and security staff
- Qualified sports staff.

Pros and cons

This is the glamorous side of the industry, but you have to be prepared to work extremely hard in the run-up to an event. A venue may not be available until the night before to set up your stand, so you work through the night. As we go to press the EU Directive on workers' hours doesn't have much effect; most people enjoy their job so much they accept that working at a glamorous event usually means long hours.

ADMINISTRATION AND ORGANISING STAFF

CASE STUDY

ForEx (Foreign Exchange) is vital for international business. Up to 4000 dealers meet frequently for conferences in different countries. Lukie worked for Cunard when ForEX came to London.

'I was in charge of 125 interpreter/receptionists speaking ten business languages. In the six months leading up to the conference I had to book freelance staff to work the five days of the conference, ensure there was the right mix of languages, design and buy uniforms, brief the staff and write a working manual.

'I needed IT skills to organise the shift rota, send out confirmation letters and update requirements. Almost every week there was a meeting with the clients to be updated on what was planned for delegates, accompanying persons programme, meals, venue, and VIP guests. When staff were needed to meet delegates at Gatwick or Heathrow airports I had to contact many of the staff to see if they were able and willing to start work a day or two before the conference opened. After meeting delegates, these staff accompanied them into their hotels, then took them to the opening ceremony.

'Some staff started before the conference opening, sorting out badges and delegates' kits. During the conference some staff were working on information desks issuing badges and conference literature to delegates, while others went with the accompanying persons (usually partners) when they went off to visit stately homes and museums. After the conference was over there were thank you letters to write, staff to pay and lost property to be restored to delegates – then on to the next conference, which was dealing with cardiology.'

INTERPRETERS AND TRANSLATORS

Exhibition and conference papers need to be translated. Every major international conference will need its simultaneous interpreters (giving a translation as the speaker is talking), and international exhibitions will employ reception staff speaking languages. A degree in modern languages is a start, but to be a simultaneous interpreter you have to take a specialised course. The International Association of Conference Interpreters (AIIC) can give more details (see 'Further information').

'BACKROOM' STAFF

These are the 'humpers and doers', and can be drivers, carpenters, electricians and lighting experts, builders and logistics experts. It is their job to get the show on the road, which can involve taking an exhibition stand and its component parts across Europe, including paperwork for Customs and Excise. On-site there is a tight schedule to set up a stand for an exhibition or rig up a complete stage set for a concert. Generally crew work for specialist firms and are hired out by their company to organisers. Ex-Forces personnel are often in demand. If you can move tanks across Europe you know how to move 40-ton vans full of expensive equipment!

IMPLANTS – TRAVEL SERVICES

Many large companies have an 'implant' – someone employed by a travel agent working in their office or factory to provide travel services for their staff only. Usually trained in a travel agency, they will have taken ABTA's Association of British Travel Agents' Certificate (ABTAC) qualification. Travel geography is essential as a firm's staff will be travelling the world; so is an agile brain that can plan a complicated itinerary which may have to be totally changed at the last minute.

STEWARDS AND SECURITY STAFF

Events always need stewards to marshal crowds, show visitors to their seats and sell programmes. Security staff cover everything from checking and patrolling venues to guarding celebrities.

SPORTS STAFF

Anyone with a sports qualification can often find work with tour operators who take teams to play abroad. Jobs are also available with incentive companies that organise team-building games for companies, and hosting visitors at sporting events.

More jobs in conference and events

'Executive' is a job title that covers a multitude of roles in conference, exhibition and event organising companies. Events can be a royal opening, a pop concert, a visit during the Tall Ships Race, an agricultural show etc, either in the UK or abroad. Many exhibitions are held abroad, in one country, or on a cycle going to a different country each year. International roadshows featuring pop stars are often organised by British companies (we have the expertise).

Staff can be involved from the initial market research to test the viability of an event, contacting sponsors, mailing potential delegates or visitors, selling stand space for an exhibition, receiving and processing conference and concert bookings, preparing catalogues or programmes, booking speakers, and opening personalities etc. During the event executives ensure it runs smoothly, supervise temporary personnel, solve problems, and check health and safety issues. Afterwards there is the 'wrap up' where everything has to be put away, taken down and returned to owners, thank you letters written, and planning started for next year's event.

Temporary staff are often needed in this sector. Working as a 'gofer', demonstrator, interpreter or information staff can often be a way into working for a company full time.

Incentive travel

Companies often give staff a sales target; reach this, and they are taken away for an exotic holiday paid for by the firm. Incentive travel companies will employ full-time executives (under lots of different names) to sell and service this type of promotional holiday. Marketing and business administration skills are useful. These companies also need freelance tour managers to look after the winners on behalf of their company – usually one person per 10–20 winners. Languages and an OCR (Oxford, Cambridge and RSA) Diploma are useful.

Training

Some people start working in the sector straight from school, and learn 'on the job'. Others enter after taking a marketing or business management degree. First-aid and the OCR Diploma for tour managers are useful; IT skills are vital for admin work (see 'Further information'), and languages are very useful.

Where to find jobs

The Association for Conferences and Events (ACE), Corporate Hospitality Association (CHA) and the British Tourist Authority (BTA) publish lists of members (see 'Further information'). These cost from £15–£25 and are a good starting point when looking for jobs. Your local Tourist Board will have a list of business travel members. Major conference and exhibition venues such as Earl's Court, Scottish Exhibition Centre and NEC Birmingham publish lists of forthcoming events with names of organising companies.

Are you suitable?

You must be smart, articulate and have plenty of stamina. Languages are useful. Financial training from bookkeeping upwards can be an asset. 'Backroom staff' such as drivers and builders have to be flexible about shift working, as much work is overnight.

Chapter 2
HOSPITALITY

'Hospitality' is the umbrella title for hotels and restaurants, and it is probably the oldest sector of the tourism industry. Innkeepers have been providing beds for travellers since the time when Joseph and Mary had to make do with a stable because of over-booking. Today the industry is better regulated (in most areas) and provides millions of jobs worldwide. This sector is so large that there is another book in this series devoted to it – *Getting into Hospitality* (by Beryl Dixon, published by Trotman).

Here we cover some of the job opportunities that have come about because of a shift in trends, and which are not included in *Getting into Hospitality.*

To find the top jobs paying mega-salaries you have to work, work and work. When faced with earning a huge salary, or running your own show, most people say that they forget the EU Working Time Directive. As an executive you love the work, and are such a perfectionist that you can't leave work until everything is in place.

Types of job

- Catering manager for corporate hospitality events
- Manager for town house hotel
- General manager for international hotel chain
- Restaurant owner/chef.

Pros and cons

These jobs can be high profile. You might meet celebrities, VIPs, politicians and the press as well as the general public. You will be earning a good, sometimes a *very* good salary. Generally you have to travel a great deal, promoting your hotel ('property') or company at international fairs and events. This can also be a problem, as you struggle to catch up with sleep after jet-lag, knowing that tomorrow you start off again travelling to another international event.

Expect to work 18 hours a day six or seven days a week. When one internationally famous hotel manager announced he was bringing his wife and children to a reception, cynics expected them to be wearing name tags so he could identify his family.

Working your way up can sometimes be extremely stressful – and even worse when you reach the top. Anyone who watched the recent TV documentary on Chef Gordon Ramsay would have heard him shouting more bad language than you might hear on the football terraces (possibly because he is an ex-footballer). Yet he has no lack of applicants to join his brigade in the kitchen. Even one waiter who had been dismissed for drinking from a bottle of water in view of customers, admitted on camera that perhaps he was 50% to blame. The old adage, 'If you can't stand the heat, get out of the kitchen' applies to top kitchens. Good chefs are artistes, and artistes are noted for short tempers!

CATERING MANAGER, CORPORATE HOSPITALITY

CASE STUDY

Timothy works for a corporate hospitality catering company, arranging events where 'blue chip' companies entertain their clients.

Timothy always enjoyed organising things – from family picnics to planning surprise meals for his sisters' birthdays. Leaving school he took a degree in finance and administration, expecting to 'be something in the City', but fate took a hand.

'Up the road was a major stately home that often hosted corporate hospitality days. A company would take over the house and grounds and invite top clients to spend a day at this impressive venue. The day was organised as a 'thank you' to clients, keeping their loyalty so that they would buy more of the company's products.

'In my final year I was home for the holidays when I met the stately home's agent looking for staff to help out serving drinks and food at a corporate hospitality day. I liked the money being offered, so said I would turn up in "black and white" (black trousers and clean white shirt – standard waiter's uniform).

'Arriving on the day I found chaos – the van bringing the chairs and tables had got stuck in a flood, and there weren't enough seats for everyone to watch the falconry display or sit to eat lunch. The owner of the house was looking distinctly uneasy at the thought of his Chippendale chairs being used instead.

'I whizzed into gear, suggesting that as the day was billed as "a day out in the country", why not offer the guests just that? Get the estate tractors to haul in some of the old wagons and place these around the park where the display was to take place for people to sit or stand on. Then set up straw bales as seats for lunch. With a few artistic touches, when the guests arrived there was a very upmarket picnic area laid out which everyone thought was great fun. It helped that the sun was shining, and the straw bales looked almost elegant on the lawn in front of the house.

'The caterers were impressed, and their boss asked me for my telephone number. The next day there was a phone call – would I be interested in helping in one of their marquees at Wimbledon? I wouldn't get to see the tennis, but would be well paid. I liked the money offered, so accepted. Two weeks later with blisters, tired eyes and aching feet – I knew that I would be able to contribute to the company, and asked for a job. As it turned out, they had watched my work, and were about to offer me a job.

'I went on to work at the Veuve Cliquot Polo Championships at Cowdray, the Grand National and lots of other sporting events. Sometimes I actually got to see the event, but the work was so interesting it didn't matter if I missed it.

'I now work as an account manager. My assistant and I meet clients, listen to what they want, and then come up with suggestions for entertaining guests. Then it is back to the office to work out costings (where my financial training is invaluable) and put together a proposal. If the client accepts, we then work out a schedule for organising the event.

'My job takes me all over Britain, and sometimes abroad. It can be tiring and demanding – but never dull.'

MANAGER, TOWN HOUSE HOTEL

CASE STUDY

International hotel chains became popular when travellers realised that these hotels always had en-suite bathrooms, working telephones and business centres. Today, with these facilities to be found in most hotels, guests look for something more personal and individual. Hence the rise of the 'town house hotel'.

Penny works as a duty manager for a town house hotel in London's famous Knightsbridge. The hotel is popular with guests as it offers charming individual rooms with business services, and lots of extras that make guests feel pampered.

'I was offered the job before the hotel opened, and had great fun going around with the owners picking and choosing the "goodies" for the bedrooms. The owners like dining out, so decided they would offer breakfast and 24-hour room service with luxury snacks, and then wrote a critique of all the famous restaurants nearby so guests could choose where to eat. I photocopied these, bound them and now each bedroom has a hand-written restaurant guide.

'I like jogging, so I devised a jogging trail map. Each guest bedroom has a map, plus a Walkman with a selection of tapes to play while taking exercise. A rain storm one day sent me out negotiating a deal for umbrellas for all the bedrooms – and I am always on the look-out for more touches to personalise the rooms.

'Each morning I am on duty in the entrance hall, chatting to guests and saying good-bye to those leaving. It is quiet during the day, giving us time to confirm reservations, do the accounts and write to suppliers. At tea-time it is back into the hall to welcome guests and explain about the honesty bar system, where guests can help themselves and write down what they have taken. Believe it or not, guests are always honest. Most evenings there is a lively session where we introduce guests to each other, while they have a drink and decide which restaurant they will visit.

'The night manager comes on at 8pm, and I go home. Normally I work four 12–13 hour days in a row, then have three days off.'

GENERAL MANAGER, INTERNATIONAL HOTEL CHAIN

CASE STUDY

As general manager for one of the world's top hotels, Peter finds every day is different. To reach his current job, he worked his way up from Swiss hotel training school, via jobs in Hong Kong, Miami, Paris, Munich and Rome. He has worked everywhere but home, which is London.

Swiss hotel training schools are very expensive, but the training is excellent. Most tuition is in English, to ensure that students speak the language. They have to wear a proper suit in class – not trainers and T-shirts. A bonus is that each class has a network system where classmates keep in touch with each other. Often, if there is a job vacancy one of his mates will phone Peter to tell him – that is how he was offered his current job.

'My hotel belongs to a very exclusive chain of international hotels, and each property has its own character. The company expects their general managers to operate their hotels as if they were their own – and it gives me a very generous salary package with share options.

'Each morning I tour the hotel, meeting the staff and keeping an eye on what is happening. I greet Toni, the concierge, who speaks six languages and is an invaluable member of the team. Toni wears a crossed keys badge on his uniform lapels, denoting he is a member of the prestigious Clefs d'Or (Golden Keys) fraternity. This is the association of the world's top concierges. Part of his job involves knowing where to get Concorde tickets for guests when the plane is overbooked, which is *the* newest restaurant, and where to get tickets to just about anything.

'I chair the daily meeting of department heads. They tell me what the room occupancy was the previous night, any major repairs that might be needed to furnishings or rooms, alert me to any special guests who are expected, and remind me if there is a Royal or Presidential visit when I must appear in tail-coat and striped trousers to greet them.

'Then it is back to the office, going through projections for the next two years, approving budgets, talking to builders about the ever-present problems of maintaining a luxury hotel in a pristine condition. Then I take time out for a game of tennis in the grounds. I insist on having time to exercise – I've got to be in tip-top physical condition if I am to work long hours.'

RESTAURANT CHEF

CASE STUDY

One of the people Peter has working for him is Sam, the executive chef. Only 25, Sam is about to get his first Michelin star for the hotel restaurant's food. Chefs today are stars in their own right, and Peter knows the publicity that surrounds any Michelin award will bring predators around, offering Sam his own restaurant. At the next meeting with the hotel financiers Peter will have to persuade them to offer Sam a big salary increase to keep him working for the hotel. But it will be worth it if it brings in more customers.

'I probably work even longer hours than Peter. I am up early to go to the markets to choose fresh meat and vegetables. There is another chef in charge of breakfast, leaving me time to start food preparation for lunch. A short break afterwards gives me time to check accounts in his office, before going out into the kitchen to start the preparation for dinner.

'Unlike Peter I've never taken any courses, except for health and safety training. I always wanted to be a chef, and when I was 14, I knocked on the door of the local restaurant, asking to be taken on as a vegetable chef. Even hours of peeling and chopping potatoes, carrots and other veg didn't put me off. Luckily my boss saw my dedication, and I soon started moving up in the kitchen hierarchy.' Sam doesn't decry training, but believes that experience is as valuable for many people – in a recent survey half of the top chefs said they had received professional training, and the other half had learnt on-the-job.

He is good looking (although he doesn't think so), and TV and newspapers are always interviewing him. He soon realised that if he wanted to save up enough money to start his own restaurant, he had to become a 'personality' to bring in customers. He hopes he will soon earn his first Michelin star, and then it's off to start up on his own. One of his regular clients has offered to finance him – but he doesn't know how to break the news to Peter.

Training

Once you had to go abroad for the best training, but schools such as Butler's Wharf School for chefs and restaurant staff (0171 357 8842) now offer excellent training.

The Hospitality Training Foundation has an information pack (090 6844 3322). Switzerland still has some of the world's best hotel schools (contact Swiss Hotel Schools Association: 00 41 79 402 7777). Tuition fees range from a few thousand up to £25,000–£50,000. No, it's not a misprint, but students are prepared to pay these sorts of fees because the training gives access to some of the very best jobs. For Sommeliers there is the new school at Vinopolis – City of Wine (0171 645 3700).

Where to find jobs

Ask at the kitchen door. Contact up-market hotel groups. Schools such as Butler's Wharf say their students walk out of the door with a job, as employers contact them with good offers while they are training.

Are you suitable?

Only you know that. You must be flexible with regard to shift work and hours, although when you first start working in most hotels and restaurants hours will be much shorter than our case studies.

Chapter 3
LOOKING AFTER PEOPLE

These jobs involve receiving and looking after clients, such as meet-and-greet staff who work at airports and transport links, representatives, tour managers and guides.

Types of job

- Meet and greet
- Representatives
- Guides
- Tour managers.

Pros and cons

If you like meeting people, this is the job for you. Travelling with clients, generally you are treated extremely well. You are being paid to see the world. Conversely, if something goes wrong it is up to you to sort it out – the head office is usually a long, long way away. You may have to work 24 or even 36 hours non-stop if there is a strike or delay. If someone is unhappy about their holiday, *you* – as the company's representative – have to take their anger. It is no use saying 'I'm not paid to listen to you.' Sorry – you are – and however rude or verbally abusive clients become, you are being paid to sort out problems. If you don't like it, you can resign. Or you can realise that rudeness is often caused by jet-lag, and the following morning clients will be back to their usual friendly selves.

The work is seasonal, and when you start you must ensure that you have some temporary job you can fall back on while you become established. One good aspect of the influence accountants have (because they organise hotel financing), is that hotels, cruise companies, airlines and coach operators now stay open all year round, rather than closing during the off-season – so offering more work. Many people in this sector work for promotions, conference and exhibition companies in the off-season.

MEET AND GREET

Airlines need meet-and-greet staff, as do major tour operators to check in people and meet clients on arrival. There are some specialised jobs such as working for the Foreign and Commonwealth Office as an 'Escort' (only a government office could get away with that as an official job title!) Languages help with this type of job.

REPRESENTATIVES

These are the people who represent a company at a resort, in a city or particular area. If you watched the TV series on holiday reps, or that docu-soap 'Sunburn', well, the industry is not like that. Work is much more about customer contact and giving customer care, carrying out administration, slogging between hotels and villas to meet clients, and waiting around at airports for delayed flights. But this job is probably the best training for working in the industry. Most chief executives of tour companies started as reps.

CASE STUDY

Sally works for an up-market tour operator which organises tours for Americans wanting to visit Egypt. She works in London, meeting clients who fly in on their way from the US to Egypt.

'Unlike most people, I am employed full-time. This has been a blessing recently with all the multiple cancellations because of political problems. Now the situation seems calm, so I am back to meeting clients off the plane from New York. Tours start in London, because the British Museum has the world's best Egyptian section. On the "budget" tours I meet clients at Heathrow in the early hours of the morning and take them to an airport hotel. They have a short rest, then we go by coach into central London to visit the British Museum. My degree covered ancient history, and I love guiding here. Then I take the clients back to Heathrow where they fly out to Cairo on an evening flight.

'Sometimes I also work as a tour manager for the luxury tours, meeting clients off Concorde, then taking them into London to stay at an exclusive hotel. The following day we visit the British Museum, then might have dinner in a private house whose owner has an interest in Egyptology. Next day we fly out to Cairo (first class – even me!) to join a luxury boat cruising the Nile. Sometimes these can be tremendous fun, with a wonderful "house party" atmosphere. Sometimes clients can be a bit of a pain, and I have to ensure that someone who has had an argument with a fellow passenger sits well away from them during dinner.

'There are lots of compensations; no one ever forgets Son et Lumiere at the Pyramids, and I can understand why the Aga Khan chose to be buried on one of the world's loveliest islands in the Nile.'

Campsite representative

One growth area has been in campsites. Forget the old image of Boy Scouts putting up tents in a windy field. Today's clients have their tents ready erected, or stay in mobile homes. Companies need representatives based in areas all over Europe, able to greet clients and see them into their accommodation, handle problems and organise excursions. Some companies will employ husband and wife teams.

Children's representative

If you are under 20, this is one of the best ways in to the industry. The job involves organising a varied programme of daytime and evening activities for groups of children from 2–12. You must have experience looking after children, and preferably an NNEB or NVQ in Childcare.

GUIDES

There are guides for all sorts of tourist venues – stately homes, museums, sites of special interest, plus trail guides in parks, walking tour guides, 'interpreters' who explain the history of a site, and registered guides who are official guides for an area, town or city.

CASE STUDY

Once travellers on holiday would stay somewhere for a month at a time. Today everything is condensed and visitors may only spend two or three days – sometimes less – visiting an area. Valerie works for a company that looks after overseas visitors wanting a 'quick, in-depth look' at an area; a contradiction if ever there was one!

'My company offers study tours to teachers, and I find the work absorbing. The downside is that I have to do a lot of research in my own time to find out information about, say, the Huguenots in London or silversmithing. Both are subjects of recent study tours. The plus side is that I get to meet the most interesting people: tourists and locals. My last group went on a day trip from London to Oxford, where we were met by the Keeper of the Western Archives. A wonderful old title, with a mega-intelligent holder who kept us enthralled explaining about the books that belong to Oxford University. Even I was impressed, and my visitors were speechless.

'For every job I check the details the day beforehand, which can mean phoning to check we are expected, confirming lunch times, and organising to pick up entrance tickets from the office. I arrive half an hour early at the group's hotel, and hopefully I will have been able to talk to the tour leader beforehand to find out what interests everyone. It is always more interesting if you can bring in something personal on a tour.

'Sometimes I work just in London, perhaps in the Victoria and Albert Museum, rather than touring round – where all you can see is the rear view of the coach in front. Huguenot history is my speciality, and this museum has a particularly good selection of some important Huguenot pieces. It is important to tailor the historical comments to the interests of your group, and with the Huguenots I get the group (who are usually quite wealthy!) to open their wallets and get a £50 note to look at. Why? Because Houblon, the founder of the Bank of England, was a Huguenot.

'During the day, if anything goes wrong I have to sort it out. Problems could range from ordering a vegetarian meal for a visitor, to arranging ambulances and hospital stays if someone falls ill. My day is usually 8–10 hours long, and although is it freelance work I cram in about 250 working days a year.'

Ski guide

Don't be taken in by this term – there is a difference between recognised ski guides and winter reps. The latter will meet clients at the airports, take them to their hotel or chalet, and show them where to find the lifts, where to get equipment and tell them about the nightlife. A qualified ski guide, on the other hand, has to take a rigorous course to show clients around the pistes, and, for example, should be able to advise on weather conditions. If you want to do this work, ask at an Alpine resort's TIC for details of local training courses, or contact BASI (see 'Further information' section).

TOUR MANAGER

CASE STUDY

Ben was always interested in history, and loved the lectures on Hannibal and Wellington when training for the Army. Unfortunately he was invalided out of the Forces, so looked around for work that would use his historical knowledge. The Army Resettlement office paid for him to take an OCR [Oxford, Cambridge and RSA] course for Tour Managing.

'I was told to apply to companies that ran Battlefield Tours, and when I looked into this I was astonished to see the variety. Tours ranged from two-hour visits to Brompton Cemetery in London where 14 VCs are buried, up to tours of the Iberian Peninsula following Wellington's campaigns. People want to see where battles took place, from Alexander the Great's Asia Minor campaigns to the Falklands.

'I applied to over 40 companies, and eventually, as I speak Italian, I was offered two tours to Italy: one covering World War I campaigns, and the other the British Army's advance up the Italian mainland in World War II. Luckily the company didn't seem to hear about the time I directed the coach driver the wrong way in fog on the motorway, and we ended up in Milan rather than Turin – it took hours to drive back, but the passengers were most understanding.

'I am now regarded as an "Italian specialist" and have been researching the part played by dogs as pack animals in World War I. Each tour is different, but I am a member of my company's top team, so that although the work is freelance, I earn about the same as I would in a full-time job.'

Training

- Welcome Host basic courses run by Regional Tourist Boards. Phone 0181 846 9000 for details of your nearest Board.
- Courses for OCR (Oxford, Cambridge and RSA) Diploma for Tour Managers and Guides – 0171 351 4434.
- Basic Distance Learning courses are run by Leisure World – 01295 273574.
- For Regional Guide courses for Registered Guides contact your local tourist board.
- First aid, or at least a basic emergency aid course, is vital.

Where to find jobs

These are to be found at local stately homes, in parks, factories open to the public, etc. More and more conferences now include 'accompanying persons tours' and they need guides. One growth area is in walking tours, and many towns and villages in Britain now offer these. If your area is interesting and hosts visitors, you could ask the local hotels or tourist information centres if you could organise walking tours.

Are you suitable?

You must like people, have an enquiring and retentive mind, and plenty of stamina. Languages are useful as long as you speak them well enough to deliver a commentary.

Useful contacts

It is difficult getting work at the start, so it is useful to belong to associations where you can network to obtain work. The Tourism Society (0171 834 0461) and ACE (Association for Conferences and Events – 01480 457595) both have useful student memberships. Once you have some experience join the International Association of Tour Managers (0171 703 9154).

Chapter 4
MUSEUMS & ATTRACTIONS

Once you visited a museum as part of a school visit or you were dragged there by parents who took you to learn more about the world. Today people who run museums have to go out and attract visitors, and put a great deal of thought into entertaining visitors, as well as providing interesting information.

Visitor attractions are also in the business of enticing people, especially families, to go through the turnstiles. Sometimes stately homes are also attractions in their own right – when the Duke of Bedford opened Woburn Abbey to the public, the first thing he learnt was that he needed to install loos – and the attractions came later. To entice and entertain the public, these venues employ public relations and marketing staff, designers, archivists, historians, stewards, ride attendants, shop staff, maintenance staff, builders and engineers, cashiers, programme sellers, cleaners, catering staff and car park attendants.

Museums need room stewards, warders, curators, etc. At venues with special entertainments there is seasonal employment for entertainers, actors and 'animators'.

Some jobs are seasonal, some full time. Behind the scenes there are often huge departments dealing with finance, security, safety and administration. The publicity department will often employ several people designing, writing and proofreading leaflets, brochures and booklets.

Then there are organisations such as Centerparcs whose purpose-built villages are attractions in their own right, employing over a thousand people at each park in a wide variety of roles.

Pros and cons

This is a much more structured sector of the tourism industry than most, especially when working for the household-name companies. Although marketing and public relations staff may work long hours at exhibitions promoting their venue, generally hours in administration jobs are 9–5. Working on the 'public' side is more often seasonal, with shift and weekend work.

PRESS OFFICER

CASE STUDY

Madame Tussaud's is one of the most famous venues in the world. Started by the woman whose job it was to model masks from the heads of aristocrats beheaded in the French Revolution, it is now part of a giant entertainment company.

As guests wander round the rooms, they may marvel at the models and their clothes, but probably have no idea that behind the scenes is a hive of activity. Wig-makers, dress-makers and modellers spend hours making each figure.

Carla works as here as Press Officer. Although Tussaud's is the top visitor attraction in London, it only stays that way by keeping its name in front of people, and providing information for journalists so they write about new attractions.

'I bring out fascinating facts to capture people's attention. Did you know that when Tussauds make a model of Queen Victoria, they use clothes that actually belonged to the Queen? Even down to her underclothes. Silk stockings are easy to find; Her Majesty only wore them once, and then they were given to a Lady in Waiting. Her Majesty's voluminous knickers are a little harder to find.

'There is a black dress that we know Queen Victoria wore 14 times because there are 14 sets of pin-holes from her favourite brooch. This is the sapphire and diamond brooch Albert gave her, and today it is often worn by the Queen.

'PR for an attraction isn't all curious facts – there is a lot of hard work, but it is always interesting.'

ROOM STEWARD

Stately homes and museums employ staff called room stewards, whose role is part security, part providing information to the public. They are generally appointed to one room or gallery.

RIDE ATTENDANTS

At theme parks and attractions, the rides need staff to collect tickets, check visitors on to the ride and operate safety checks.

Training

First-aid and health and safety courses are most important. The English Tourist Board's Welcome Host is a good introductory course. Other courses are the English Tourist Board Tourism and Hospitality Diploma (0181 846 9000) and the OCR (Oxford, Cambridge and RSA) Course for Guide Training. For administration jobs, people with degrees in finance, marketing and business administration are in demand.

Where to find jobs

Think private railways... heritage attractions... stately homes... local museums... theme parks. There is an endless variety of opportunities throughout the UK.

Are you suitable?

Enthusiasm is very necessary, and so is an ability to communicate with different visitors of different ages. An enquiring mind is also useful because visitors ask all sorts of questions. Many jobs at visitor attractions are outdoors – where it can be freezing-cold one day, and boiling-hot the next, so tolerance for changing weather conditions is a plus.

One good thing about this sector is that as venues make themselves more accessible to disabled visitors, they realise that there is potential to offer work to those with disabilities. Alton Towers say they are 'committed to offering equality of employment based on ability to do the job'. Warwick Castle used to have a wonderful guide who was blind.

Useful contact

ALVA (Association of Leading Visitor Attractions) 0171 222 1728.

Chapter 5
NICHE TOURISM & CONSERVATION

This is the fastest growing sector in leisure tourism. The traditional two weeks' holiday sunbathing abroad has given way to tours catering for people's special interests. Following a hobby, adventure, or a desire to see how people live and experience other cultures, gets people booking tours catering for niche tourism. Interest in conservation and a realisation that sitting on a man-made beach and sleeping in a concrete high-rise block does nothing for the locals, has radically changed tourism in the past 30 years.

In Britain ABTA used to be the overall body that upheld standards for tours. Today it has been joined by AITO (Association of Independent Tour Operators). In the past decade AITO has grown from a few small companies that offered tours for niche markets, into a giant organisation with around 200 companies in membership.

The British Tourist Authority has overseas offices that try to promote holidays in Britain. More and more staff find they are asked to suggest holidays that take in hobbies and special interests. These include tracing ancestors, embroidery, sport, railways, bell-ringing, calligraphy, military history, fashion, antique hunting – the list is endless.

One good thing about this type of niche tourism is that it gets people away from what the trade calls 'milk run' tours. These follow the same routes in every country, their coaches nose-to-tail with those of rival tour companies.

Types of job

- Administration staff
- Representatives
- Tour managers
- Conservationists.

Pros and cons

This is a rapidly developing sector, so you must have enthusiasm to explore new areas. However, if you are a dedicated conservationist you have to realise that what you might want to conserve, locals might want to tear down. So you must be an expert at compromise. Remember – those unsightly TV satellite dishes on mud huts are bringing the wonders of television to the locals.

ECOLOGICAL ADMINISTRATOR

CASE STUDY

Tommy works for an international hotel chain as Ecological Administrator. His work takes him around the world, auditing 'green' practices in their properties.

'I went to Edinburgh and took a degree in Environmental Geography. It was a very new subject, and I found it frustrating that we were filled full of theories, but not actually in touch with what was happening in the real world. My aunt, who works in tourism, started to send me brochures and packs – and one from Alp Action was particularly interesting.

'Alp Action's founder, Prince Sadruddin Aga Khan, was United Nations High Commissioner for Refugees, and decided when he retired to do something to stop the world destroying itself. In Switzerland he saw how the modern world was destroying the fabric of life, often from pollutants carried from many, many miles away. So he founded Alp Action, and using his circle of friends and acquaintances managed to make companies donate money to major projects for preserving the environment. As an example, Clarins, the cosmetics company, funds a project across the Alps to restore meadowland to enable butterflies to continue breeding. It has now adopted the butterfly as the company symbol.

'In my second year at university I contacted Alp Action sponsor companies, and was taken on by a hotel group to work on their environmental audits. One project was to study how much washing powder was used in their laundries, and our team managed to not only save the company a considerable amount of money, but by reducing soap powder and changing to a more "friendly" product, hotels are helping the environment. Now we are auditing fruit and vegetable buying. Those monster strawberries with no taste were the first to go. Talking to guests I found that they would prefer local fresh produce rather than products that had to be flown in from other countries.'

Training

Working for a tour operator, marketing and financial skills are useful to add to your interests and abilities. Courses and degrees in conservation are increasing, and gradually these are gaining credibility.

Association of Independent Tour Operators

AITO was the first major British association to take up the cudgels for environmentally friendly tourism. Working together with tourist boards, ground handlers and hotels, their tour operator members like to employ staff who have the same ideals.

All the major hotel chains and tour operators now have an Environmental Audit department, and this is spreading to smaller companies. As guests become more aware of the environment and the damage that can arise from insensitive tourism development, the more they are demanding that hotels and tour operators treat resources in a sympathetic manner.

On the Continent, people are even more aware of environmental pollution, and are determined to do something about it. When BA launched its 'Well Being' programme, German clients forced staff to serve orange juice in jugs – they don't like cartons. On some German trains, families can book sound-proofed family rooms so fellow passengers aren't disturbed by noise, and instead of a general rubbish bin on their trains, there are five separate bins for rubbish to be sorted into bottles, paper, etc, at source.

Children play their part; in Turkey a large hotel company wanted to build a vast hotel on a beach where loggerhead turtles lay their eggs. Continental children rose up and made their parents protest and the hotel company pulled out.

Where to find jobs

Contact AITO and ask for a copy of its brochure (0181 607 9080), then look up companies that offer tours where you have a specialist knowledge – destinations such as Belize and Guatemala, South Georgia and Namibia, Faroe Islands and Ukraine. AITO 'hobby' holiday tour operators offer tours for those interested in fencing, glacier walks, orchids, polo, horse riding, textiles, trekking, wolf and bear watching – the list is endless.

Are you suitable?

Do you have a passionate interest in your hobby? An incurable enthusiasm for unusual holidays? A practical approach to conservation? Yes? Then of course you are suitable.

Chapter 6
SPORTS TOURISM

Often people who play sports want to continue when they're on holiday. Sometimes they may only practise the sport when away, such as skiing and snowboarding. Or they may go on holiday to take up a new sport, such as sailing.

Sometimes they take short break – a day or weekend – to see a special event such as horse or motor racing, or international athletics. Or a sports team might want to travel and play against other teams.

Active holidays are increasingly popular; among the most popular today are flotilla holidays. An operator will base several yachts in an attractive part of a coastline, and offer week-long tours to people who want the fun of sailing but are not confident enough to go off on their own. One yacht will have an experienced skipper and crew who are there to shepherd their flock around the coast. Each day the yachts set off and if there are any problems they can contact the skipper on the radio.

Other activity holidays are riding breaks – both in the UK and on the Continent – and tennis clinics where clients stay for one or two weeks in a resort and have lessons every day. Whatever the sporting activity you are interested in, there is likely to be a holiday based around it.

Types of job

- Administrator
- Tour manager
- Representative
- Guide.

Pros and cons

Enjoying a sport will keep your interest alive as you watch with your clients. However, you may not get the chance to play – you are just set for a game when one of your group has a problem – guess who has to sort it out? Yes – you. And bang goes the game you lined up. Working at major events such as international competitions and the Olympics may sound fascinating, but it could destroy any ideas you have about taking part in a sport for the love of it.

The most difficult part of sports tourism is organising home teams to play matches with visitors. There are many groups that want to travel as a team, hoping to play against other teams. However, most teams have their calendars organised months or even years in advance, and fitting in another game can be extremely difficult.

CASE STUDY

Susan was good at gymnastics, and represented first her club, then the county, and finally England at competitions. While abroad she got talking to an American coach who wanted to know if it would be possible for his team to come to Britain for international competition practice.

'When I returned home I asked around, and found everyone in the club was very excited at the idea of actually having an American team come to our gym – and perhaps a return visit back to their homes. My mother was wonderful. She asked around our friends and came up with 20 families who were willing to host one or two members. Then our National Association became involved and the Regional Tourist Board, and 18 months later there we were waiting at Heathrow to meet our guests.

'The whole visit was a great success, and now our club has an annual visit. One year we go to the USA, the next the Americans come to Britain. Having retired from competition, I made use of my contacts and work as an administrator for a tour operator that organises exchange visits for sports clubs. This involves finding an area where there are enough pitches, courts or whatever. Then there must be enough local families who are willing to host overseas visitors. Although they are paid for this, it needs someone dedicated to look after the guests, and today with both parents working in so many families it is difficult to find people with the time. Or we have to find a suitable Youth Hostel with adequate facilities.

'Then I have to find teams that are willing to play in competitions. Overseas teams like to come here to play hockey, netball, rugby, swimming, tennis, fencing and many other sports. My company is now thinking of expanding into providing sports for parents, such as golf and riding.'

CASE STUDY

Sports often form an important element in incentive travel tours. Although incentive travel is business travel dedicated to providing services for companies that want to award staff who increase sales etc, taking part in a sport is an exciting way to reward those who reach their sales targets.

When Garth was deciding on a career, he was convinced he wanted to go into advertising. Taking a course in Media Studies, he went for work experience to a tour operator. As a reward he was offered a spare place on the company's luxury coach trip to the Cowdray Gold Cup – polo's version of a Cup Final.

'I don't know anything about horses, but it seemed churlish to refuse, especially as everyone else thought it a great honour. I must admit the five-course lunch in a special marquee was brilliant. Imagine eating a meal cooked by a top London chef, with Veuve Cliquot champagne to drink!

'The game was fantastic. I was rooting for the home team, sitting on the edge of my seat watching this incredibly fast game where players use a small mallet to hit the ball over a hundred yards. The horsemanship is unbelievable – I reckon the players must use superglue to stick to the saddle. I was totally exhausted when the final hooter blew.

'Coincidence often makes up my mind. I remembered the name of the company that had organised the day at polo, and when a friend told me this company were looking for someone to work as a tour manager, I decided to give it a go. It was a good move; the work is great fun; last month I was busy organising a trip for an advertising agency to Switzerland. They were taking some of their best clients to play 'mini-Olympics', with races on a ten-man ski, and dog sledding. That was the bit I liked best – those dogs just pull their hearts out, they love their work so much.

'One evening we were to have dinner in a mountain restaurant which could only be reached by snowcat. I was talking to the dog kennel owner, who told me that he had enough teams to take everyone up the mountain by dog sled. So I suggested to my boss that we substitute the vehicles with dogs. There was enough float money to do this and insurance was in order. So we changed the programme to pick everyone up by sled, and the clients were delighted as they sped up the mountainside.

'Magical. Until I came back to the office and had to reconcile all the expenses for the client's invoice. Just because work is fun, doesn't mean a programme runs itself, and it my job to check out things like insurance, qualifications of those staff we use for the sports content in a programme, and reconcile the invoices at the end of a tour.'

Training

Marketing courses are extremely useful. The Royal Life Saving Society runs training in lifesaving and lifeguarding (01789 773994). Lifeguarding is mandatory for certain jobs in sports tourism. It is also useful if working as a tour leader with groups, as most sports programmes will include a visit to a swimming pool. You will need training in first aid. There is an OCR Diploma for Tour Managers.

Where to find jobs

There are companies that specialise in handling sporting groups. Ask the governing association for those in which you have an interest. Incentive companies often look for someone with an interest in an 'up-market' sport such as golf, sailing, polo, tennis, etc.

Are you suitable?

You have to like hard work, have an interest in sport and be enthusiastic.

Chapter 7
TOUR OPERATORS

Tour operators put together the elements that go to make up a 'package' holiday. This usually consists of transport, accommodation and and/or services such as transfers, guided tours, etc. There are three distinct tour areas: outbound operators, which send tours overseas; inbound tours which are tours coming into a country; and domestic tour operators which organise tours inside their own country.

Types of job

- Brochure production
- Contractors
- Customer relations
- Finance
- Marketing
- Product development
- Representatives
- Reservations staff
- Sales staff.

Pros and cons

There are a lot of administration jobs in all sorts and sizes of companies, which might include several of the jobs listed above. If you like a structured life, working in an office of a major tour operator can give you more defined job responsibilities and perhaps more regular hours. However, if you like to 'muck in', working for a smaller tour operator where everyone has two or three job titles and responsibilities might be more interesting.

BROCHURE PRODUCTION

Every tour operator needs leaflets or brochures to sell their holidays to customers. Small companies may use freelance designers and production houses; large companies will have a complete department devoted to year-round production. Photographs have to be taken of properties, descriptions written up and checked, then proofs have to be sent out to the city or resort to be checked for accuracy. This is very important as the EU Directive on Package Travel says customers can demand compensation if a description is inaccurate.

CONTRACTORS

Contractors negotiate with hotels, villa owners, self-catering apartments, airlines and coach companies on behalf of their company. Hotels publish rack rates (the room rate the general public will pay). It is the contractor's job to negotiate with the hotel owner to bring this rate down. They do this by suggesting that by selling room allocations in bulk to their company, the hotel won't have to do any promotion or marketing, won't have to produce a brochure, won't have rooms unlet if someone doesn't turn up, and will have a guaranteed income to show bank managers. All the hotel needs to do is give the company a discount. That is the beginning of negotiations that can last long into the night!

CUSTOMER RELATIONS

In a small company this is handled by anyone from the managing director downwards. Large companies have a complete department devoted to customer relations, and an interest or a degree in Law can be useful. The job involves replying to letters of complaint, researching reasons for complaint, advising if something needs changing, or perhaps suggesting compensation. Unfortunately many people almost make a profession out of complaining, and try to get money out of a company in devious ways – so employment in this sector is likely to rise.

FINANCE

This is probably the most important department or section. When organising travel and tours across frontiers, tight budgetary control is vital. Many companies rely on clients purchasing their holiday months before they take it; the interest earned on their payment helps tour operators make money. Companies need to buy currency forward (this means purchasing foreign currency before it is actually needed, in case the pound loses value) and there is an art in guessing what the markets will do. It is very easy for a company to lose money when exchange rates fluctuate; delays can mean extra expenses; and legislation means more complicated and therefore expensive handling. In many companies the finance director is next in seniority to the managing director.

CASE STUDY

David went out to Spain to learn Spanish. Like all students he needed to make money, and found a job working as a transfer rep for a local ground handler looking after clients of a British tour operator. As his Spanish improved, he did more and more work for the operator. Eventually he was offered a full-time job in another resort where they had an office.

'It has taken three short years to work my way up to negotiating with the hoteliers on behalf of my company. Eighteen months before the clients arrive, we start talking to hoteliers. Forward projections have told us how many rooms we need to contract, although we have to be flexible in case of good/bad weather, or other factors that can affect bookings.

'I spend days negotiating with hoteliers in Spanish; just a few pence off a room rate can make the difference between a profit or loss. All the time I am in contact with my Head Office, and every so often the team will arrive with the financiers to talk to hoteliers, their bankers and solicitors. No contract is signed until after an enormous amount of haggling. Afterwards there's usually a big dinner given by the hotelier to celebrate. It is surprising how the hotel owners who have pleaded poverty can suddenly lay on the most magnificent banquet once the contract is signed!

'Then it's quiet until next year, so I work in the office supervising the 50 or so hotels we use. I am constantly on the go, but have a company car which I can use on my day off to explore the "unknown Spain" behind the Costa del Sol.'

MARKETING

Most tour operator employers will place a marketing qualification at the top of their 'wish lists' when hiring staff. In a marketing role you have to organise the promotion of your company's product or service to potential clients. This can involve a number of duties, such as writing press releases, undertaking PR and representing your company at conferences and trade fairs.

PRODUCT DEVELOPMENT

Product development is the department that searches out new hotels, resorts or countries for the company's tours. In a small company this could mean keeping your eyes open when you go on holiday; big companies have teams to research holidays for different market segments. Languages can be very useful.

REPRESENTATIVES

Reps are an important part of most companies' workforce and we cover their work in Chapter 3.

RESERVATIONS STAFF

In a small company you may know your clients personally – they return so often they have become friends. As companies increase in size so do their reservations departments, until in the major companies you may be working in a call centre miles away from the public. Staff sell holidays, take the bookings and send confirmations.

SALES STAFF

This is more fun than it sounds; sales staff visit travel agents in the 'off season' to promote their company's holidays, telling agency staff about new destinations etc. They may organise evening functions to promote their tours – usually an event such as a disco.

CASE STUDY

Working for a major tour operator, Steve, Tina and Dan have to plan events to keep their company's name in the minds of travel agency staff.

'We work well as a sales team, putting together a road show that goes around the country to tell agency staff about new developments. We carry out a blitz in targeted areas; either areas that traditionally produce a high percentage of bookings, or areas our marketing department identifies as having potential to produce more sales. During the day we will visit agencies, leaving extra brochures, perhaps putting up a window display featuring our company, and talking about familiarisation trips for staff to visit our resorts so they can experience our product at first hand.

'At least one evening during our visit we will run a disco for the young – and not so young – agency staff. As we are taking up their free time we try to make it fun, while putting over the company message.

'During the evening we will have a quiz based on our holidays. There are lots of give-aways to keep everyone's interest, and one very good prize to be won – everyone is on their toes to win this. Then it's on with the dancing – and after a hard day's selling it can be tiring to pretend wild enthusiasm for the latest hits until 3am!

'During the season we may help out with reservations and go on familiarisation trips to get to know the product.'

Training

Qualifications in sales and marketing, finance, business administration, and art and design are all useful. ABTOC (ABTA Certificate) is administered by the Travel Training Company (01483 727321).

Where to find jobs

There are three major employers' associations: ABTA, AITO and BITOA (British Incoming Tour Operators Association). Their members generally have employment opportunities, but these do depend on the size of the company, and what skills and knowledge you have to offer.

Are you suitable?

Apart from representative work, these jobs are basically office work, with the added bonus that when you visit an office to check paperwork it could mean hopping on a company plane to Spain or Turkey. Office work means that you have a more structured working week, and with some jobs there is very limited contact with the public – but you may prefer that. You will need office skills such as being able to use computers and good organisation and administration.

Chapter 8
TOURIST BOARDS

Tourist boards are set up to bring inward investment into a region, by promoting the area to leisure and business visitors. Staff give out information, market the area, provide press and public relations, publications and produce brochures. Some boards have in-house photographers, film and radio producers, training and administration staff, all dedicated to helping members and promoting tourism venues to visitors. Tourist board staff in contact with members of the public generally need to speak English and at least one other language fluently.

Types of job

- Brochure production
- Information assistant
- Marketing
- Press officer
- Training officer.

Pros and cons

Many boards are funded partly or completely by government money. When politicians become involved it can be unsettling for those working in this sector. The UK government has recently focused on this industry as an area of job creation for the unemployed. Unfortunately, if time is not taken to understand the industry, job creation doesn't happen – and the pattern is to regain credibility by cutting tourist board funds. Workers in this section are constantly on a seesaw.

On the plus side you are being paid to promote scenic and interesting areas, and there is a chance to work abroad for the British and other National Tourist Boards. If you are a national of another country there may be a chance to work in London for your country's Tourist Office.

BROCHURE PRODUCTION

All visitors want information, and even with so much available via the Internet, most people like a colour brochure in their hands. These brochures are usually produced in-house, often by the marketing department, although the larger tourist boards may have their own production team with designers, photographers and copy writers.

INFORMATION ASSISTANT

There are over 800 TICs (Tourist Information Centres) across Britain operated under the umbrella of the English Tourist Board (ETB). Many local authorities and tourist venues also operate TICs. Languages are very important; to work in a London TIC you must be able to speak two languages fluently, plus English. Outside London you will need one language plus English. Sales skills are useful as you will have to sell books and maps, and learn to operate the BABA (Book a Bed Ahead) reservations scheme. Some TICs are only open during the season, while others open all year round.

CASE STUDY

Nigel works for a TIC in a country district. When he started the job was seasonal, but recently the local authority has allocated funds for Nigel and a colleague to keep the TIC open all year round.

'Everyone imagines that TICs deal with foreigners, but I would say the majority of our clients are British people, with a large proportion being locals who pop in to book tickets for concerts and find out about the next sheepdog trials or organised "town walk".

'I am glad the town walks are popular. When we were told the Council had allocated funds for year-round opening, I realised that we would have to justify our existence and bring in funds to top up the allocation. In the back of my mind was the idea that when you live in a district, you like to know what is going on, but sometimes don't know the history. So under the strap-line "Know Your Town" we started running a walking tour once a month just for locals.

'The local paper and radio covered the first walk, and from a shaky start we now have enough interest to be able to run these once a week. We soon realised it was taking too much of our time to sell to individuals, so we target schools, OAP groups and local societies.

'Any spare moments see us filling the brochure racks. Local attractions pay us a fee to distribute these to visitors, and often pop in to make sure their racks are kept filled. Sometimes I could swear the leaflets walk out of the door on their own.

'Our TIC is affiliated to the English Tourist Board network, which runs our training courses. Once trained, we are kept up-to-date with one-day seminars on everything from "Increasing your profits from BABA" to "How the Working Time Directive will affect you".

'But with all our training, the most popular question our TIC has to answer is "Where are the toilets?"'

MARKETING

Governments of many countries will subsidise a tourist board, whose main purpose is to encourage visitors. Most look enviously at Australia's budget; it allocates up to ten times as much as some countries to attract tourists. The investment is paying off with the number of visitors to Australia rising each year.

CASE STUDY

Working for a regional tourist board in England, Lisa sometimes looks enviously at the other stands at exhibitions. Her board takes space to promote the region, with membership fees helping to pay the huge marketing costs.

'I took a Marketing degree at the local college, but project work just didn't prepare me for the reality of having to find creative ways of stretching the tourist board's marketing budget. It is my responsibility to promote the various companies we have in membership – such as stately homes, B&Bs, hotels, restaurants, theme parks, museums, a cathedral, lots of shops, and individual guides – to potential visitors. Visitors could be individuals, or groups brought in by tour and coach operators, incentive travel organisers and associations that might want to make a visit to our area.

'To do this we send out brochures, attend exhibitions, seminars and conferences, and in conjunction with the press office we try to get as much mention as possible on TV, radio, in magazines and newspapers. I also work with the information officer to update our information line. We have had to go over to an 0891 telephone number for enquiries. We and BT share the income from this line, which helps pay for the brochures that enquirers request.

'I would dearly love to produce four-colour glossy brochures to show off our beautiful scenery, but this would cost too much. Instead, we have to be creative to encourage visitors. One way is to target children with giant cut-out figures of a nursery rhyme character created by a local author, by the side of the roads at the entrance to our area. Attract children, and they will bring their parents so we get the adults too!

'It took days of my time negotiating with the Department of Transport for permission to erect these figures on private land. Luckily the local conservationists said our figures would be an improvement as they replaced some grotty adverts already there, otherwise we would never have been given permission.

'The art and design department at the local college produced the characters with wood that we found in the tourist board's garage, so it didn't cost us anything more than a few drinks and sandwiches when the first one was unveiled. Now our characters feature on all the brochures, and make an eye-catching display at tourism exhibitions.

'Exhibitions are an important item in our budget, where we talk to the trade – coach and incoming tour operators, associations, group organisers and tour managers – to give them all the details of group rates, coach parking, new attractions and anything else we can think of to encourage visitors. Exhibitions often mean an early morning start (3 or 4am) taking our "characters" and a portable exhibition stand. It always takes longer than you think to erect the stand, and usually exhibitions start at 10am.

'Then we spend all day answering questions, and taking enquiries to funnel out to our members when we return. By the time I get home it is often midnight, and then I have to face getting into the office early to deal with the mail from the day before. (Secretary? My predecessor's part-time assistant was taken away with the last government cuts.) Then it's down to making sense of all the requests I scrawled down at the exhibition, and telling members who wants what information.

'In my job I learn to be creative on a small budget; we never know when the government may withdraw funding for the English Tourist Board, which would mean our board's allocation would be cut down. All of us have in mind an escape route to another job, just in case we find our job has been "downsized". However, with the contacts I make in my job I am not too worried, and I really enjoy meeting all the different tourism personalities in the area, and promoting their services to incoming visitors, both British and from overseas.'

PRESS OFFICER

Press officers keep the media up to date with developments and events in the area. When journalists write about a destination, however well they know the region, they generally go on a press trip to see what is new, or changed, and the press officer will be responsible for organising the visit.

CASE STUDY

Terry is Press Officer for a local government authority. Realising that a factory that was a major employer in the area was about to close down, the local authority did a feasibility study on tourism potential. This came up with several plus points that could be promoted to visitors, and Terry was appointed as Press Officer.

'Yesterday morning I met a journalist who arrived the night before to stay in one of our luxury hotels. We always try to fit journalists into suitable accommodation. This one writes for an antiques magazine, which we know attracts an upmarket readership, so chose an appropriate hotel. She wants to see cultural sites, plus some "more unusual venues". So the first stop was to see our Swannery. This is unique; has been here for over 500 years, and swans gliding up and down with their cygnets make for unforgettable photos.

'We spent far too long talking to the staff at the Swannery, who all have interesting stories to tell, and had to rush off to the next stop; meeting the curator of the county museum. This has some fine 16th century silver, which the magazine readers will appreciate. Then it was off to lunch, which featured the latest restaurant to gain a Michelin star. The staff are very professional, and totally understood when I said firmly that we only have *one hour* for lunch; 55 minutes later we are drinking coffee and contemplating the chocolates – both of us succumb.

'Walking off lunch we headed towards the Cathedral, and I pointed out its unusual features, including misericords with devils and other gruesome figures that will delight children. You learn quickly in this job – a year ago I wouldn't have had an idea what these were.

'Afterwards we visited the local stately home, which has some interesting furniture. I left the owners and the journalist talking about Chippendale, and used the time to phone my office to confirm arrangements for another press trip next week. Then it was a mad dash to the station, the journalist just caught her train – and I got back to the office to attend to the post, and hope the day will result in a good article that will bring more visitors to the area.'

TRAINING OFFICER

There are two sides to this job: organising day courses for members on everything from new legislation to marketing their properties, and training the local Tourist Information staff to answer the public's queries. Training updates for tourist board staff are also organised in order to keep up with developments in tourism.

Training

The English Tourist Board's 'Welcome Host', 'Welcome Host International' or 'Welcome All' make good introductory courses. Its Tourism and Hospitality Diploma is a popular course based on the needs of employers. Visit its website: www.careers-bta.org.uk for more information. Marketing courses are generally very useful.

Where to find jobs

Contact the nearest TIC; they will be able to give you addresses of local authorities and regional tourist boards.

Are you suitable?

You need to be methodical, but with a flair for marketing and publicity. It is important that you get on with people. And you should have good writing skills to be able to write reports.

Chapter 9
TRANSPORT

Travelling to your destination is an important part of a leisure or business visit. Airlines, railway and coach companies, ferries and ships all need staff.

Trains revolutionised travel in the last century, and have come full circle a hundred years later. Until Eurostar came along, train travel had become cheap transport for students, pensioners and the 'anorak brigade'. Suddenly, this incredible machine has become a star performer in its own right. The north of France and Belgium has opened up to the weekend break market, and business travellers think nothing of hopping on the next Eurostar train – as they would take a local train to a meeting. Airlines and ferries have become more competitive to encourage more bookings.

In Europe it was the French TGV system that revitalised rail links. Now there is Thalys, which is a joint venture between the rail companies of France, Belgium, Netherlands and Germany, providing high-speed trains across Europe. British business and leisure travellers are realising that seamless travel by Eurostar, linking up with TGVs and Thalys at their hub station at Lille, can provide an alternative to the stresses of airline travel. One reason why Eurostar is doing so well is that staff pay is good – when it first opened staff came over from the airlines, and now there is no trouble in recruiting top employees. There is also more work with the low-cost airlines formed to counter this competition.

Pros and cons

If you suffer from motion sickness, this work won't be for you. If you have to travel across date lines you can get jet-lag, which can cause small but annoying health problems. Shift work is the norm, and delays can extend working hours. But you are paid for travel, and during your time off you can explore other cities and areas.

1. AIRLINES

Types of job

The TV docu-soap 'Airport' was well-received by the industry. It highlighted the types of jobs and staff needed to run a large international airport, such as:

- Administrators
- Air traffic controllers
- Customs and Excise staff
- Immigration officers
- Architects, engineers, builders
- Retail staff
- Airline receptionists and passenger service agents.

International airports are like small cities. There are jobs for staff in administration, and anyone who saw 'Airport' will have seen the work that administration staff carry out, from sending off aircraft from the ramp, to running a terminal. Air traffic controllers are needed to marshal aircraft as they fly into and out of their air space; Immigration, Customs & Excise staff work at all airports with international traffic, airports are constantly expanding, so they need architects to design termini and builders and engineers to build them. One of the fastest growing job areas is in airport shops. Today, airports rely on the income received from these shops to subsidise landing fees.

Visit your local airport to see what jobs are available. The Information Desks usually have excellent leaflets giving more information about the airport, and the information assistants should be able to tell you where to apply for jobs.

PASSENGER SERVICE AGENTS

CASE STUDY

Airlines need check-in staff, generally known as Passenger Service Agents, to handle their passengers. They are often helped during busy times by freelance staff like Debbie.

'During my college holidays I applied to the Heathrow Job Centre and was offered a job working for an American airline as a Passenger Assistant. This is a grand job title for handling queues. When passengers arrive they have to go through security checks and then wait in a queue to be checked in. To make sure passengers are in the right place it is my job to go up to everyone and help them find the right queue. Join the wrong queue, and by the time you reach the top you may have missed your flight.

'I check passengers' tickets, and then show them which queue to join. I have to have eyes in the back of my head to make sure no one queue jumps. Luckily we have guide ropes to contain the queues, but it can become very heated in July when we are overwhelmed by people going on holiday.

'During a shift I am on my feet all the time, and keep a spare pair of shoes and extra tights in my locker. Changing into these half-way through the shift makes my feet more comfortable. We have to wear uniform, and the uniform shoes were very cheap and uncomfortable. We have negotiated a shoe allowance instead, and I pay about £120 a pair for my court shoes. This makes a hole in my budget, but it is worth it to be comfortable.

'I have been offered a job as a Passenger Service Agent for my company, and this will mean I will sometimes work at the business class or first class check-in. There it is calm; carpets on the floor and no queues! Still, those passengers are paying ten to twelve times as much as people in economy class so I suppose they deserve their privileges.'

2. COACH TOURS

Types of job

- Coach driver
- Guides working in an area or city (generally returning to base each evening)
- Tour managers: in charge of the administration of a tour, as well as giving commentaries during the trip (generally they stay with their group in hotels each evening)
- Traffic managers: in charge of administration in a coach operator's office. They need to hold the OCR Certificate of Professional Competence (CPC).

TOUR MANAGER

CASE STUDY

Tour managers travel in charge of coaches, looking after tour operators' clients. The job involves administration, being good at customer relations, especially when sorting out problems, and being able to give interesting and informative commentaries as the coach travels along. Generally the job is freelance, which suits Carole.

'I like working for myself, and as a freelance I can choose when I work. Starting out, it was difficult to get work at first; I had been warned about this, and using the jobs list I was given on my OCR course, I phoned and phoned, wrote CV after CV, and just as I was thinking of giving up, the first company phoned back and offered me a tour.

'This was a weekend break to a Christmas market in Germany. Reality was very different from their advertisement. We had to start at 5am in order to pick up all the clients. Then there was a long wait at Folkestone before we got on Eurotunnel. Arriving in France there was fog all the way across Belgium, so we arrived very late at our hotel near Cologne.

'Next morning the sun shone (although it was freezing) and everyone enjoyed themselves walking around the market. That evening I was told to sell a company excursion to a wine cellar – and was surprised that everyone bought a ticket, so the driver and I earned good commission.

'By the time we arrived home at 1am I felt I had really earned my fee – but I can't wait to go back next weekend!

'Over the year I earn enough for a comfortable lifestyle. When tour operators phone to offer me a tour, I check my diary and if I'm free the operator faxes over the itinerary. This is so I can start revising the information I need for commentaries. I spend hours in the local library looking up facts and figures; reading everything I can find to provide amusing pieces of information that will intrigue and inform passengers.

'Before I start a tour I have to sort out paperwork and collect the float to pay for entrances and a multitude of services to be paid out on behalf of the tour operator's clients. I will need lists of passengers, and rooming lists giving any special requirements such as diet or easy access needed because of a disability.

'Then it is off to meet the group. If it is a long tour with clients from the USA and Canada I fly to Paris or Amsterdam to pick up the passengers, then off we go in a German or Dutch coach; I speak a little Dutch and lots of English to the Dutch drivers, but I speak fluent German so use this language to talk to the German drivers. We usually try to speak a language that passengers don't understand – otherwise they are so curious that all our chat gets broadcast between passengers across the coach.

There are very few women drivers – it's not sexist, just that having to lift those ton-weight suitcases the Japanese and Americans bring with them causes havoc with women drivers' internal muscles.

'I have to keep to a strict timetable in order to be able to fit in all the visits; passengers hate being hurried, so this is where tact comes in. When we arrive at our hotel in the evening I rush round checking everyone is in the right room, that dinner is booked and the right menu being cooked. Otherwise every hotel would serve chicken, chicken and more chicken.

'Although I am on my own, there is a network of colleagues doing the same job for different companies. After I had worked for two years I applied to join the IATM (International Association of Tour Managers) which keeps us in touch with changes in legislation, ferry times and those obscure places with the wonderful views for photographs.

'After dinner it is off to my room to go through my paperwork for the next day, make phone calls to confirm the hotel arrangements, confirm the guide and check opening times for a museum. My bed-time reading is more guide books – I have over 800 at home and am still learning – but I love my job.'

GUIDE

CASE STUDY

One of the fastest growing sectors in leisure tourism is walking tours. People no longer want to drive past interesting countryside. They want to get out and experience walking through vineyards and battlefields; see old villages at first hand, and meet locals. So they go on walking tours, but these are very different from the old-style holidays where people had to carry heavy rucksacks and stay in hostels.

As soon as they retired. Charlie's parents took off on a vineyard tour. They came back raving about the experience, and it sounded so interesting that Charlie decided to take an OCR course and applied to a tour company. He spoke fluent French and Italian, and had worked in a wine shop during his holidays. He had taken a course in Business Administration, and during the holidays he worked for a champagne house in France giving guided tours to visitors. He enjoyed the work but decided that after one season, he had had enough of telling basically the same story every morning and again in the afternoon. So he decided to work for a tour operator taking tours around an entire wine district.

'The company put me through a rigorous training course, where I learnt everything from basic first-aid to remembering to take lots of plastic bags. Why? To issue to smokers on their tours, so they could put their butts inside and not litter the countryside.

'I work with Mario, an Italian. Each morning we get up early to buy provisions for a picnic. Then I set off with the group to walk through Tuscany. Mario loads the passengers' luggage into a mini-coach and sets off to a pre-arranged picnic site. Once there Mario sets out the food, ices the wine, and waits for the group to arrive at midday. He tries to provide different food each day that is typical of the region – and the group are always eager to try the specialities.

'After a long leisurely lunch, Mario and I then ask who wants to continue walking. Those who are tired can opt to go in the coach with Mario who drives directly to the next hotel. The rest amble off with me, and I tell them about local life and culture, point out interesting features in the landscape, and give an informative and amusing account of local history.'

The hotel is always the best in the town, and when they arrive any passengers go off to their rooms to rest, while Mario cleans the coach, then relaxes by the swimming pool. Soon Mario hears the rest of the group arriving with Charlie, already discussing what they are going to eat at dinner. Didn't they appreciate his picnic lunch?!

Charlie says he has enjoyed his tour managing and guiding, but has decided to make use of his Business Administration course. 'There is a vacancy in Head Office, and I am going to apply. I will still get to go on walking tours, but this time I will be a passenger, checking them out. I want to experience every facet of the operation, as it is my ambition to set up my own company one day.'

3. CRUISES AND FERRIES

Cruises and ferries are a fast-expanding sector of leisure tourism, and they need a range of staff.

Types of job

- Catering and hotel staff on both cruises and ferries
- Pursers' staff with secretarial skills for administration
- Entertainers
- Sales staff.

PURSER

CASE STUDY

Jo works as an Assistant Purser on a cross-channel ferry.

'Living in Dover, I had always seen the ferries plying backwards and forwards. During college holidays I took a job working in a shop on board a ferry. Most ferries and cruise liners need sales staff to work in the souvenir and sometimes duty-free shops. Then there is work for cleaning staff, or stewards and stewardesses, and cabin staff to keep the ship clean and provide cabin services. While I was there I had to deal with a nasty emergency. A pregnant passenger developed complications; luckily I had taken a first-aid course, and as I was nearest I took over.

'When we arrived in France the doctor said she had to go straight to hospital. I speak fluent French, so the Purser said to go with her to help if I could. She wrote a glowing letter to the company, and the upshot was next year they wrote to ask if I would be interested in working in the Purser's Office for the season.

'My job ranges from helping the Purser complete the company paperwork to answering passengers' questions. These include the mundane – like "what time is it?" – and complicated queries about dealing with visas.

'We work a shift system, 24 hours on the ferry and 24 hours off. This can be changed if there is a storm – one shift lasted three days. We had to run for shelter right down to the Channel Islands. The passengers were lifted off by helicopter, but we had to stay on the ship to prevent looting. It is no use doing my job if you get seasick!

4. TRAINS

Types of job

- Conductors/customer service agents
- Drivers
- Catering staff.

CUSTOMER SERVICES AGENT

CASE STUDY

Eurostar is a premium railway service needing top people working at its main termini in Brussels, Paris and London. Staff are also needed at the intermediate stations at Ashford and Lille. Staff must speak fluent French and English, and other languages are very useful – many nationalities travel by Eurostar. There are opportunities to transfer between the various locations, and staff on board the train regularly stay overnight in one capital or another.

Francine is a French customer services agent married to an Englishman. 'Working for Eurostar at Waterloo means we can travel frequently to Lille to see my parents. But this is a bonus; I actually took the job because the whole concept was so exciting. It may be strange for a woman to be excited by trains, but when the sleek trains glide into the station with a "whoosh", I think it's thrilling.

'We wear a very smart uniform, designed by Balmain, so we are easily identifiable. Customer services agents working at Waterloo assist passengers by showing them the way to the platforms, helping them put their tickets into the machines to gain access – some are so laden with luggage they hold the ticket in their teeth and expect us to take it out of their mouths and put it through the machine. Ugh.

'We have regulars – business travellers who take the train out at 6.58am and always have a cheery word for us. They are travelling to Lille or Paris for meetings. Then there are the lovers – Eurostar seems to have a sexy image and has become extremely popular for trips to Paris. You wouldn't believe the stories we hear from the catering staff – talk about joining the "mile under" club.

'Like all transport, Eurostar did at first suffer from under-use during the day, but now that we have a tie-up with Disney, off-peak trains are filled with happy families. They are so excited – grown-ups as well as the kids. We are kept on our toes answering questions, but it is all good fun.

'Sometimes we have to provide a VIP welcome service, particularly for foreign ministers, and sometimes princes and kings. Travelling between Paris and London, their security staff like the seamless travel, so tend to book whole carriages for their charges.

'I am thinking of applying to be a train manager to work on the trains, supervising seat allocations, handling problems and making announcements. I live within one hour's travel of Waterloo, and speak French and English fluently. I was bought up in Northern France near the Belgian border, so am brushing up my Flemish and then I'll apply.'

Training

Training will depend on the sort of job your are considering and which of the transport services it is in. Here are some suggestions.

- **Cabin Crew:** contact ATA (Airline Training Association) for details of colleges offering NVQs (01494 445262 – a small charge is made for your call) . In addition you will have to take each airline's individual training programme. This is because aircraft configuration is different, and in an emergency you have to be able to find emergency exits, etc. Passenger service agents can take the OCR course.
- If you want to be a **pilot**, unless you have been trained in the forces, you will probably have to pay for your own training. This is expensive, and it would be worthwhile investigating training in USA, where it is cheaper.
- Working as **air traffic controllers** is regulated by CAA (Civil Aviation Authority) who can advise on training (0171 379 7311).
- **Customs & Excise** (01702 367888).
- Hotel training is useful for work on ferries or cruise liners, as is secretarial training for pursers.
- **Tour managers and guides:** OCR (Oxford, Cambridge and RSA Certificate) course; Regional Tourist Boards sometimes offer guide training courses. NVQs are being developed and offered in colleges, but do check that the college is offering industry-approved training, and hasn't just jumped on the tourism-training bandwagon.
- **Coach companies:** first-aid. Drivers need to have a clean driving licence, weight in proportion to height and good eye-sight. They have to take a Passenger Carrying Vehicle (PCV) test. The Chartered Institute of Transport can advise on courses for traffic managers.

Are you suitable?

Obviously you can't suffer from motion sickness! You must enjoy meeting people and be able to work shifts – sometimes long hours. Languages are important in most jobs where you will be travelling to other countries and many of the passengers are non-English speaking.

Chapter 10
YOUR OWN BUSINESS

Pros and cons

At some time or another, everyone wants to run their own company. The grass is always greener on the other side, and it seems so easy to tell people what to do, especially when you know what clients want and would like to set up a company to supply it. Then you come up against all the legislation that constricts companies today.

It is estimated that 2000 extra pieces of legislation have been developed since the present government came in to power. Add to this all the legislation already in place, and it is not surprising that company directors feel they are on a treadmill constantly shuffling paper.

If that doesn't put you off, then you may be able to make a go of running your own business in tourism. The industry is full of SMEs (small and medium-sized enterprises) offering services to other companies, such as organising tours to unusual destinations, booking conference venues, offering individually tailored days out for incentive travel, or perhaps an interpreter and guide service.

Legal advice

Your friendly local lawyer just doesn't know enough to unravel the complexities of the EU Directive on Package Travel. So it is well worth while investing in a session with experts who can tell you what you need to start up: licences, bonding, etc. Alan Bowen was the person who represented ABTA when the EU were doing their best to draw up an incomprehensible directive, and is able to interpret the essential information you need to know. (He's got a sense of humour too.) Call him on 0181 908 1795. Nicholson Graham and Jones are solicitors who specialise in travel and tourism help for companies (0171 648 9000).

Government help

People are divided about this; it can work for some, yet be a tiring and frustrating exercise in bureaucracy and paper shuffling for others. Perhaps it should be likened to the curate's egg – good in parts.

Business Link has an 07000 number which only a government department could offer to small businesses; this is a top-rate call charge! But you can phone them for one-tenth the charge on 0345 567765. They say they promote the 07000 number 'because it is easy to remember'.

In Northern Ireland contact your Local Enterprise Developmental Unit (LEDU) 01232 491031 and in Wales Business Connect 0345 969798.

Training and Enterprise Councils (TECs) should be able to give information on training both for people wishing to start and business, and for those already up and running. Find the telephone number in your local directory.

Local Enterprise Agencies (LEAs) can also advise on starting up a business. Again, the telephone number will be in your local directory.

If you need to take a training course there are Career Development Loans (0800 585505). Loan applications are supposed to take ten days – users say three months is a more realistic time frame.

CASE STUDY

According to someone who managed to get government funding to start a tour operation, the trick is to apply as soon as a new scheme is announced. Daphne says the government claims it is keen to help tourism companies start up, but doesn't actually understand the industry! However, it may be possible to obtain an interest-free loan of up to £5000 for a viable new business – and a tourism company should qualify. Contact Business Link for more information. They can also advise on courses (often free) to help you with the financial aspects and organisation when starting up a business – but it takes time.

'Wait a bit, and you may find that you are at the back of a queue. I did manage to wade through the voice mails and wrong extensions at Business Link to get advice on aspects of running an SME – they offer a range of services to do with financial management, marketing and advertising – the A–Z of business. This is a single access route for information on planning permission, employment law, etc and can point enquirers to the best place to find what they want.

'By chance, one of their advisers said something about being in an area that qualified for Regional Assistance, and this triggered off an enquiry for funding. However, the time and paperwork involved in obtaining a grant would not have been cost-effective for a large company. As I worked on the forms at night, filling these in only cost me cups of coffee.

'The Federation of Small Business and the local Chambers of Commerce are not government aided, but for their small membership fees I found them very helpful. And I found it very useful to be able to network with like-minded people at meetings.'

Gizmos

If you need to buy IT equipment and office 'gizmos', and are travelling abroad, you might be able to take advantage of the BAA Information Line (British Airports Authority) on 0800 844844. Every so often, in conjunction with suppliers such as Dixons, BAA runs promotions where, if you are flying to certain destinations, it guarantees not only to pay the VAT on equipment such as laptops or fax machines, but will deliver the goods to your office or home. Don't ask me how it works – just phone quickly before the EU stops this.

CASE STUDY

Working from home means no more 'office genius' to help out when your computer goes berserk. Shaun runs a company offering tours of London's pop music scene.

Computers

'When I started, I bought a computer, and always having used a PC at work, I thought I knew it all, until something went wrong. That was when I realised I couldn't lift up the phone and get a company expert down to sort out the problem.

'Now when I buy any gizmos my first questions is about their helpline. Is it based in Britain, or will I have to deal with someone who may speak my language, but is not on the same wavelength? Is there a local helpline number, or will I spend a fortune having to "hold on"?'

Phones

'Telephones are vital, and I have investigated companies that offer cheap calls, but there is one big problem. If you sign up with some providers and there is something wrong with your telephone, they have an appalling engineering service.

Some won't take reports from callers – they insist that only the registered number holder can report a fault! Another company has an answer phone that says "We know there is a fault in your area", when you are calling from miles away! Oftel should sort this out, but they don't.

'So I use a mix of BT and Cable & Wireless – their services aren't fantastic but on balance their fault repairs service is better than the other companies.' (BT Business Connection 0800 333300; Cable & Wireless Business to Business 0800 096 5555.)

Cordless phones

'Parcel couriers delivering music tapes ring the doorbell once, and then they are off – not waiting for you to finish a phone conversation. It sounds amateurish to ask a business caller if they can hang on – so you need a cordless phone. You can carry this to the front door, or into the garden, and no one knows. Make sure the phone is digital for clear reception. I am very happy with my Philips Onis which goes as far as the bottom of the garden.'

Mobile phones

'Cordless phones are not to be confused with mobile phones – mobiles are expensive on calls, and I soon realised talking to important clients they don't carry these gizmos; if a mobile rings in the middle of a meeting it destroys the impression I try to give of office back-up.

'However, if you work as a tour manager mobiles are essential, but make sure they can be used in whichever country you work. BT can advise on unlimited international roaming.'

Cameras

'In my job I have to give presentations to visiting groups, and soon discovered that I was paying a fortune for professionally produced slides. So I went to Olympus Cameras for advice, and they suggested a Zoom 140 camera. They gave me a tip – always use professional quality slide film such as Agfa RSX 100. You can only buy it at shops with fridges, and you must keep the film in the fridge at home. Results are stunning, and I have even had my slides published in glossy magazines. All from a simple camera that even I can operate.'

Fax machines

'I used email at the office, but soon realised that it wasn't so useful when working from home. After one visit abroad I returned to find 74 messages; only one was of interest to me, though no doubt the PR companies thought I should know all about their products. Now I prefer to have a printed fax message that I can take around with me. I have a plain paper fax from Philips which is a reasonable price and provides photocopies that are almost as good as the real thing. It also has an answering machine with a large memory which I need for overseas calls coming in during the night.'

Printers

'If you have to send out reports it is essential to have a good quality printer – laser printers generally give the clearest type.

Working from home

Many tourism companies are run from home offices. It makes sense to cut down on massive office overheads, and you can off-set a percentage of your home costs against tax. However, take professional advice, as if you sell your home you could be liable for tax.

CASE STUDY

During his holidays from university, Tom worked as a tour guide on punts. Tourists loved being punted along the river in flat-bottomed boats while he pointed out the sights. 'What I didn't like was having to hustle for clients; as each train or bus arrived in the town, my colleagues and I would meet it and try to make visitors pay £8 for our tour. If I managed to get three people for each 40 minute tour, I did well. But if I only found one person willing to go, it was difficult to make enough money to pay for the hire of the punt.

'One day a tour manager asked if I could arrange for his group to take a tour that evening. There were 42 passengers, so I rounded up all my colleagues and we had a wonderful evening, ending up taking the visitors to our favourite pubs. I realised that I could make a better living if I concentrated on groups, and so when I went back the following term, I took time out to see a bank manager to ask for a business start-up plan. All banks have them. I studied this carefully then went to the tourism officer of the university. He was delighted to see that I had planned to carry public liability and other insurance, and said that if I started a proper company, the university would pass on our details to tour operators enquiring about excursions.

'He suggested I join the local tourist board, which offers courses in marketing and promotion. Luckily I had been too busy working in the summer to spend my earnings, because these courses were expensive – and I had to slot them in between revision for my Finals.

'During the summer I noticed that my friend Sally was very good at selling, She would smile sweetly at visitors, and start chatting. The next thing they knew, they had agreed to go out in her punt. I knew that I wouldn't be able to operate a company on my own, so asked if she would be interested in coming in with me to market 'Punting Tours'. We agreed that for the first season we would work one day on the office, and one day on the punts. That way we should earn enough money to live on, and not take anything out from Punting Tours.

'Sally and I went around the colleges and told them what we were doing. We chose our tour guides carefully, and insisted they all had first-aid qualifications, and took out their own insurance. Every time we had seen a college bursar or tourism officer, we had to write and thank them for seeing us, and send our brochures.

'One evening, I was so tired, I nearly didn't write: I am glad I did because the letter I sent produced a marvellous enquiry – 120 visitors were coming to the university for a conference and the organisers wanted to offer the delegates an amusing evening function. Divided into groups of 40, one group went punting, one group were given a demonstration of how to make a cup of tea (a friend produces hilarious comedy sketches, and performed to wild applause) and the third group played a skittles match in a local pub against a group of our friends – who were only too happy to play in return for free booze, Then they all changed over.

'Realising that come the winter visitors would be scarce, Sally and I went to see local hotels to offer special guided walks for winter weekends. We belonged to the Association for Conferences and Events (ACE) and networked among organisers, which produced more work. Even so, with all the expenses of setting up, our first 18 months often saw one or the other of us working in the local pub, as we had no money coming in. After many long hours, we now have a business with potential, offering walking tours, cycling tours, punt tours and excursions for coach groups.

'We needed an office, and as both Sally and I were in student accommodation, we didn't have space in our digs. However, Sally's grandparents had a garage at the bottom of their garden. It was well built, but needed a make-over to be an office. We contacted the local council; as long as we didn't make a noise, put up advertising or live on the premises, they weren't worried about us using the garage. So we put in electricity and a telephone line, and spent all our spare moments painting it. Furniture came off skips – it's wonderful what people throw away, and how much you can use if you can borrow a supermarket trolley.

'Now our business is working well, and we are able to work full-time which means more time to go out and promote the company – and more work coming in.'

Training

New Deal is for unemployed people to be trained to work for companies. If you have been registered as unemployed for six months, especially if you are aged 18–24, you might qualify for free training. However, the take-up with this programme has been very low, probably because it rehashes old programmes, and doesn't address the problem that no matter how well-trained you are, if the jobs aren't there – you won't get one.

The Prince's Trust has had a more successful track record. Phone 0171 543 1234 for details of your local office, and information on how the Trust helps young entrepreneurs.

Local Training and Enterprise Councils (TECs) can sometimes help – again it can depend on where you work. The Welsh, Scottish and Northern Ireland Tourist Boards and English Tourist Board can provide marketing advice and surveys at a reasonable cost. Some European clients may want prices quoted in Euros. The BTA has published a guide for small tourism-related businesses. Phone 0181 846 9000 for a copy.

Chapter 11
INVEST IN YOURSELF

As readers may be working on their own – as staff, freelance or as your own boss – this is a light-hearted chapter on things like stress, erupting skin, hints and tips.

Before you start

You must have some or all of the following to offer a prospective employer:

- Enthusiasm
- First-aid – take a course with your Red Cross or St John's Ambulance
- Languages
- Flexibility – no moans if you have to work late
- IT skills for office work
- Have done work that needed 'customer care' skills.

Interviews

Depending on the company, you might have a five-minute interview over a cup of coffee, or it might take all day. Some might be group interviews to see how you react with other people, or just you with one interviewer. It's possible to prepare for interviews, and you should do so wherever possible. There are some excellent books on interview techniques and it's worth your while to research them – but if you fail an interview, remember in tourism there will be another job along shortly.

Application forms

Companies that ask you to fill in an application form place great emphasis on neatness. And that window on the back page that asks why do you want to work for the company? It's there for a reason. Someone in the office will read the front page to see if you can write legibly, then turn over to the back – and look for buzzwords such as 'customer care', 'enthusiasm', 'feel I can contribute', 'went on a holiday and thoroughly enjoyed it', etc. *Never* mention money.

Travelling to interviews

You may have to attend interviews away from home. Often companies do not pay travelling expenses, so it is worth while investigating what National Express can offer. There are student cards giving discounts, off-peak fares, mid-week travel discounts, etc. With a network criss-crossing Britain there is almost certainly a suitable service.

Networking

Abroad, tourism staff belong to the relevant trade association as a matter of course. They know that this is probably the easiest way to find a job. In Britain, we neglect this useful way in to the industry.

Most associations have student or associate membership. Take advantage of this to belong to the Tourism Society, ACE (Association for Conferences and Events), your local tourist board etc. Invest in some business cards which you can get cheaply from machines in major stations, exhibition halls and airports, and then network for jobs.

When you get your membership bumf look carefully at the list of members. Which companies might employ people like you? It can be easier to ask for a job from a member if you belong to the same association. Or you might meet a potential employer sitting next to you at the AGM.

Personal money

Coutts, the Queen's bank, advises when travelling abroad to take a selection of methods of payment such as cash, debit and credit cards and travellers' cheques. Don't carry it all together – assume it will be stolen and hide it around your person. Use safe deposit facilities in your hotel, but leave a note to yourself not to forget to claim it. And make sure you belong to your credit card's insurance scheme; if cards are stolen one phone call is all it takes to cancel the cards so no one else can use them, and these companies can arrange for money to be sent to you, which will normally take 24 hours

Avoiding poverty

These are a few tried and tested ways of finding temporary jobs when you don't have work. If you have customer care skills from working in shops or restaurants, etc, you have many of the skills that companies look for in temporary staff. Coventry Data Services (01203 426400) often needs temporary staff working at major exhibition venues such as Earl's Court and the NEC, registering visitors and making out their badges.

Promotions companies often look for temporary staff, from handing out leaflets to working at exhibitions. If you speak languages there may be work receiving overseas visitors. Contact exhibition venues, ask for their lists of organisers, then contact the organisers to find out which staffing companies they recommend to standholders.

In the autumn many cosmetics companies need staff to promote their Christmas ranges in stores and chemists around Britain. Pay and bonuses are generally better than working in shops. Buy *Exhibition Bulletin Yearbook* £25 (credit card order line 0181 313 0244) and look for companies under Demonstrators and Stand Attendants.

Field promotions need staff for temporary sales forces to promote products, from cars to washing machines. Even tour operators and regional tourist boards need these temporary staff to distribute brochures to travel agents and give a sales pitch, put up a window display, etc. You often have to be able to drive for this work. Send a large sae to the Field Marketing Association, 5 Chessington Park, Dunnington YO1 5YA for a list of field marketing companies around Britain.

Clothes

In many jobs, such as reps, cabin crews, pursers etc, you will be given a company uniform. It is up to you to keep it smart and clean at all times. One trick for women is to ask for a size too big – to stop those horrible wrinkles across the front. If you don't have a uniform, 'you can feel at a disadvantage,' according to Valerie. 'Working at conferences, I often have to attend posh receptions and dinners. Trying to keep up with the smart Swiss and elegant Italians wasn't easy until I discovered "good as new" shops. Now I can buy the most gorgeous outfits at a fraction of the price.'

Your skin

Cabin crew, conference workers, tour managers and just about everyone working in tourism (male and female) say their skin suffers from stress and travel pollution. Most say they spend more than their friends on protecting their skin, but admit this pays dividends. Knowing you look good helps you cope with long hours and stress.

There is one beauty aid that costs next to nothing: water. Cabin crew advise taking a bottle with you on long flights to rehydrate your skin. Drink as much water as you can while travelling, and when working late. Then you have to invest in good products to protect your skin.

One compensation in this job is being able to buy the latest skin-care products at cheaper prices. We mentioned the BAA's Information Line earlier – all the products you need can be ready for collection at 'duty free' prices, if you are going to certain countries.

Much research has gone in to making the right products to help us all look younger. Some companies make a special effort to come up with products suitable for travellers, and time and again staff have recommended the ones below. We cannot endorse any companies or their products, but include them here as being well tried and tested by hard-working staff.

CASE STUDY

Ella's job as a conference organiser frequently involves travel. 'I often work through the night setting up a conference, and then have to stand up in front of a large audience and hope I look good. I copy airline cabin crew, who slap on moisturiser all the time. When the Swiss firm, La Prairie, started to sell their products in airlines' first class, crews were taken by their creams, especially day and night creams. An air hostess introduced me to La Prairie's Caviar Pearls and I use these to counteract dry skin caused by stress. Their day creams contain sun-protection which is vital; many people in the tourism industry suffer from skin cancers, and I am always careful to guard against sunburn.'

The French firm Roc has simple packaging, but spends research money on producing products with a high SPF (sun protection factor) to guard against the sun's rays. Experts say that this should be at least 15, and just because you put on two products with an SPF of 15 this doesn't double the protection – 15 is 15. Lips can get very dry, and crews (male and female) carry Roc's Lip Stick with an SPF of 20.

There is no need to look pallid under all that protection, but in the past self-tanning creams had a 'sour grapes' smell. However, Ella says she uses the Roc Natural Look self-tanning lotion, which doesn't smell.

Top make-up artist Samantha says 'There are products that can fake a tan, without looking yucky', and recommends the Terracotta range by Guerlain. 'This gives a sun-tanned look without damaging the skin; clients often say their friends tell them "you do look well", when it is this make-up that covers up lack of sleep!

Supermodels have taken up the MAC range of make-up. This is made by a Canadian company that put its money into the product, rather than the packaging. Cabin crew became used to friends asking if they were flying to North America, and would they buy some MAC products. Now they are available at BAA counters and high street shops.

Arriving in Japan, airline crews are always the first to book a massage. Body massage and facials help stressed travellers and are a worthwhile investment – as is anything that can make you look good – especially in a profession where your personal presentation counts for so much.

GLOSSARY

Bonding

Under the EU Directive companies offering tours with transport, accommodation and/or services have to offer a guarantee before accepting clients' money. Major associations such as ABTA, AITO etc, operate a bonding scheme for members which ensures that clients' money is safe once they have paid for a tour, even though the operator might cease trading.

Chain hotel

Groups such as Hilton, Accor, Sheraton etc, that bring together similar hotels across the world, and market these to clients under the same branding.

Customer service

The latest buzzwords for courtesy and service – looking after customers in the best way possible.

Ground handler

A company that supplies services and looks after tour operators' clients at a destination.

Marketing

The process of publicising goods, services, venues etc, so that people know these exist.

National Park

Generally an area of countryside that has been taken over and is administered by a government or their agents.

Promotion

An event that increases the public's awareness of goods, services etc.

SME
Small or medium-sized enterprise or company.

Tourism
Business of providing travel, accommodation and services for travellers.

FURTHER INFORMATION

Helpful contacts

Some associations just do not have the staff to deal with enquiries about training or working in the industry. They now publish information packs, giving an overview of the industry, different types of job, skills and qualifications needed, and where to find training. These packs are full of information and very helpful.

If an association makes no charge for supplying information, please send a stamped, addressed envelope (sae).

ACE (Association for Conferences and Events) Riverside House, High Street, Huntingdon PE18 6SG. Send £15 for an info pack.

AEO (Association of Exhibition Organisers): 01442 873331

AGCAS (Association of Graduate Careers Advisory Services): 0161 273 4233

AIIC (International Association of Conference Interpreters): 0171 284 3112

AITO (Association of Independent Tour Operators): 01891 515948

ALVA (Association of Leading Visitor Attractions): 0171 222 1728

Alan Bowen: 0181 908 1795

Arts Council of Great Britain: 0171 333 0100

British Arts Festival Association: 0171 247 4667

Business Link: 0345 567 765

BAA Information Line: 0800 844 844

BASI (British Association of Ski Instructors): 01479 810407

Bord Failte (Eire Tourist Board): 01602 4000

British Association of Leisure Parks: 0171 383 7942

BITOA (British Incoming Tour Operators' Association): 0171 931 0601

Bus and Coach Training: 01923 896607

Butler's Wharf Chef School, 31 Shad Thames, London SE1 2YR; 0171 357 8842

CAA (Civil Aviation Authority): 0171 379 7311

CACHE (Council for Awards in Children's Care and Education): 01727 847 636

Career Development Loans: 0800 585 505

CENTAC (Centre for Education and Training in the Countryside): 01926 412427

CERT (Eire state tourism training agency): 01855 6555

CHA (Corporate Hospitality Association): 0171 278 0288

Chartered Institute of Transport: 0171 636 9952

CILT (Centre for Information on Language Teaching and Research): 0171 379 5134

City & Guilds of London Institute: 0171 294 2468

Civic Trust: 0171 930 0914

Council for National Parks: 0171 924 4077

Countryside Commission – Publications Department: 0161 224 6287; General information: 01242 521381

CPRE (Council for the Protection of Rural England): 0171 976 6433

Crafts Council: 0171 278 7700

DfEE Learning Direct: 0800 100 900 (Can locate a course or a training provider; gives enquirers information on careers information; information on funding and childcare provision.)

Department for Culture, Media & Sport: 0171 211 6200 (Although the government says tourism is all-important, it proves what it thinks of the industry by lumping it under this department's portfolio.)

EFAH (European Foundation for the Accreditation of Hotel School Programmes) c/o HOTREC, 111 Blvd, Anspach, BTE4, 1000 Brussels; 00 32 2513 6323

English Heritage: 0171 973 3862

English Nature: 01733 40345

Environment Council: 0171 824 8411

Environmental Training Organisation: 01452 840825

ESITO (Event Sector Industry Training Organisation), Riverside House, High Street, Huntingdon, PE18 6SG. Send £15 for info pack.

European Tour Operators' Association: 0171 499 4412

Forestry Commission: 0131 334 0303

Green Globe: 0171 930 8333

Guild of Business Travel Agents: 0171 222 2744

HtF (Hospitality Training Foundation): 090 68 44 33 22

IATA (International Air Transport Association): 0171 240 9041

ILAM (Institute of Leisure and Amenity Management) Lower Basildon, Reading RG8 9NE. Send £15 for info pack.

IAPCO (International Association of Professional Congress Organisers), 40 Rue Washington, B-1050 Brussels, Belgium

Irish Travel Agents Association: 01679 4089

Leisure World Distance Learning: 01295 273574 (for reps, tour managers and guides)

Learning Direct: 0800 100 900 (Details on distance learning and other courses.)

Ministerial Forum on Business Tourism: 0171 215 1079

Museum and Galleries Commission: 0171 233 4200

Museums Association: 0171 608 2933

Museums Training Institute: 01274 391056

National Association of Holiday Centres: 01608 644 824

National Express: 08705 808080

National Association for Maternal & Child Welfare: 0171 383 4117

National Business Language Information Service: 0171 379 5131

Nicholson Graham and Jones: 0171 648 9000

OCR (Oxford, Cambridge & RSA) Examinations Board: 01203 470033

Tour Managers' Diploma: 0171 351 4434

RADAR (Royal Association for Disability & Rehabilitation): 0171 250 3222

Restaurateurs' Association of Great Britain: 0171 831 8727

Royal Commission on Historical Monuments: 0171 973 2000

Royal Geographical Society: 0171 589 5466

RSA (now OCR) Tour Guides Diploma: 0171 351 4434

Scottish Vocational Education Council: 0141 248 7900

Sports Council: 0171 388 1277

Springboard, 1 Denmark Street, London WC2H 8LP; 0171 497 8654 (For information on recruitment and training programmes in travel, tourism, hotels and catering. Springboard is opening branches around the country.)

Swiss National Tourist Office: 0171 734 1921

Swiss Centre, New Coventry Street, London W1V 8EE. (For addresses of Swiss hotel schools.)

Tourism Society, 26 Chapter Street, London SW1P 4ND (Association for members and information on courses in the industry supplied to members only. Student membership £23pa.)

Tourism Training Organisation, 54a Ifield Road, London SW10 9AD; 0171 351 4434 (If writing for information of training courses, books etc send sae.)

Travel Training Company, The Cornerstone, The Broadway, Woking, GU21 5AR; 01483 727321 (ABTA's Training Company.)

UCAS (Universities and Colleges Admissions Service): 01242 222444

UK Institute for Conservation, 6 Whitehorse Mews, Westminster Bridge, London SE1 7QD

World Travel & Tourism Council, 20 Grosvenor Place, London SW1X 7TT; 0171 838 9400

Books and leaflets

ABTA's Guide to Working in Travel, Travel Training Company: 01483 727321

Careers in the Travel Industry, C Chester, Kogan Page

Dictionary for the Tourism Industry. Gives definitions of those weird words! Published by Authentically English: 0171 823 8800

GNVQ Intermediate Textbook for Leisure and Tourism, V Baker, Addison Wesley Longman. Gives a basic introduction to the tourism industry.

Good Cook's Guide to Working Abroad, Katherine Parry. Covers working in castles, villas, yachts, location catering, etc.

Handbooks published by Worksaver @ £15 each. Credit card order line 01670 789512: *Working at Conferences and Events; Working as a Rep and for Tour Operators; Working in Hotels and Hospitality; Working as a Tour Manager and Guide; Working for Airlines and Airports; Working on Cruise Ships.*

Planning the Perfect Party, Corporate Entertaining, Consilium: 01499 676 435

Training in Conservation. £3.50 from Museums and Galleries Commission, 16 Queen Anne's Gate, London SW1H 9AA.

Working in Touris, VR Collins, Vacation Work

Magazines

ACE Newsletter (members only): 01480 457595

Careerscope: 01276 21188

Conference and Exhibition Factfinder: 0181 340 3291

Corporate Entertainer: 0181 248 7711

Conference and Incentive Travel: 0181 943 5000

Exhibition Bulletin: 0181 313 0244

Group Travel Organiser: 0171 735 5058

Leisure Management: 01462 431385

Museums Journal: 0171 250 1837

The Organiser: 0171 284 2133

Travel GBI: 0171 729 4337

TTT (Travel and Tourism Training): 0171 823 8800

INDEX

Job titles featured in this book are listed in bold type below.

ABTA (Association of British Travel Agents) 5, 23, 35, 64, 70
ABTAC (ABTA's Certificate) 5
ABTOC (ABTA Tour Operators' Certificate) 35
ACE (Association for Conferences and Events) 7, 19, 60, 66
Administrator 24
AIIC (International Association of Conference Interpreters) 4, 66
Airlines 44
Alp Action 24
AITO (Association of Independent Tour Operators) 23, 25, 35, 66
ALVA (Association of Leading Visitor Attractions) 22, 66
BAA (British Airports Authority) 54, 66
BABA (Book a Bed Ahead) 38
Backroom staff 5
BASI (British Associate of Ski Instructors) 17, 66
BITOA (British Incoming Tour Operators Association 35
Bowen, Alan 52, 66
British Tourist Authority (BTA) 7, 23, 58
Brochure production 31, 32, 37, 38
Business Link 53
Butler's Wharf 13, 67
Cabin crew 51
Campsite rep 16
Career Development Loan 53, 67
Catering manager 8, 9
(CHA) Corporate Hospitality Association 7
Chef 8, 12
Civil Aviation Authority (CAA) 47, 67
Children's rep 15
Clefs d'Or 11
Clothes 61
Coach Tours 45
Contractor 31, 32
Corporate hospitality 8
Coventry Data Services 61
Cruises & ferries 48
Customer relations 31, 32
Customs & Excise 44, 51
Ecological administrator 24
English Tourist Board (ETB) 22, 38, 42, 58
EU Directives 1, 3, 48
Eurostar 43, 50
Finance 33
General manager (hotel chain) **8, 11**
Guide 14, 16, 47, 56
Hospitality Training Foundation 13
Hotel manager 10
Immigration officer 44
Implants 5
Information assistant 37, 38
International Assocation of Tour Managers (IATM) 19, 47
Interpreter 4
Interviews 59
LEA (Local Education Authority) 53
Leisure World 18, 68
LEDU (Local Enterprise Development Unit) 53
Madame Tussaud's 21
Marketing 31, 34, 37, 39

Meet and greet 14, 15
New Deal 57
Networking 60
NVQ (National Vocational Qualification) 16, 51
OCR (Oxford, Cambridge and RSA) Certificate 6, 8, 22, 30, 45, 46, 47, 51, 69
Office equipment 54–55
Olympics 28
Passenger service agent 44
Press officer 37, 41
Purser 49
Prince's Trust 58
Product development 31, 34
Representative (rep) 14, 15, 34
Reservations 31, 34
Ride attendant 22
Room steward 21
Royal Life Saving Society 30
Sales 31, 34
Security staff 5
Ski guide 17
Stewards 5, 59
Skin-care 62
Sports staff 5, 27–29
Swiss Hotel Schools Association 13
TEC (Training and Enterprise Council) 53, 58
Thalys 43
TIC (Tourist Information Centre) 38
TGV (French rail system) 43
Tour manager 14, 29, 46, 51
Tourism Society 19, 60, 69
Town house hotel manager 8, 10
Training officer 37, 42
Translator 4
Vinopolis 13
Wales Business Connect 53
Welcome Host 18, 22, 42